The Ultimate Nutella Cookbook

A Brand New Nutella Experience

By

Heston Brown

HESTON **BROWN**

Thank you so much for buying my book! I want to give you a special gift!

Receive a special gift as a thank you for buying my book. Now you will be able to benefit from free and discounted book offers that are sent directly to your inbox every week.

To subscribe simply fill in the box below with your details and start reaping the rewards! A new deal will arrive every day and reminders will be sent so you never miss out. Fill in the box below to subscribe and get started!

https://heston-brown.getresponsepages.com

Subscribe
to our
newsletter

Your Email

Table of Contents

Recipe 1: Molten Nutella Lava Mug Cake

Yield: 1

Total Prep Time: 20 minutes

List of Ingredients:

- 4 tablespoons of flour
- ¼ teaspoon of baking powder
- ¼ cup of Nutella
- 3 tablespoons of milk
- 1 teaspoon of powdered sugar

How to Cook:

1. Preheat the oven to 350°F.

2. Take an oven safe mug.

3. Mix all four Ingredients in it.

4. Put it in an oven and bake for 16-18 minutes.

5. Top with powdered sugar (optional).

Note: Let it cool off, cake has to be puffed up everywhere except in the middle.

Recipe 2: Nutella Surprise

Yield: 6

Total Prep Time: 30 minutes

List of Ingredients:

Filling

- 2/3 Nutella cups

- ½ cup or ¼ cup powdered sugar

Dough

- 2 cups of flour

- 1 egg

- 1 vanilla extract

- ½ cup baking powder

- ½ cup of butter

- ½ cup of sugar

- ¼ cup of milk

- ¼ cup dark chocolate salt

- 1 pinch of salt

- ½ cup unsweetened peanuts (almonds, raspberries, if desired)

XXXXXXXXXXXXXXXXXXXXXXXXXXXXXXXXXXXXXXXXXXXXXXXXXXXXX

How to Cook:

1. Preheat the oven to 400°F.

2. Put the Nutella and the powdered sugar in a small bowl.

3. Create 24+ balls of the mixture.

4. Place them on a plate and put them away.

5. Make a good mix of melted butter, sugar and vanilla extract and add the egg.

6. Mix to get a foamy structure.

7. Add the flour, baking powder, and the milk in which you melted the dark chocolate.

8. Create a fine, smooth and soft dough.

9. The easiest way is to spread the dough over a paper and create 24 squares (¼ inch thick)

10. At each square, place a ball of Nutella and create a ball.

11. Roll the balls into milled unsweetened peanuts.

12. Put on the baking tray and gently squeeze them.

13. All of the cookies should fit into one large sized baking
tray.

Note: The cookies will be soft when you take them out
from the oven, let them cool down before eating, just to
give them time to harden.

Recipe 3: Pumpkin Pie with Nutella

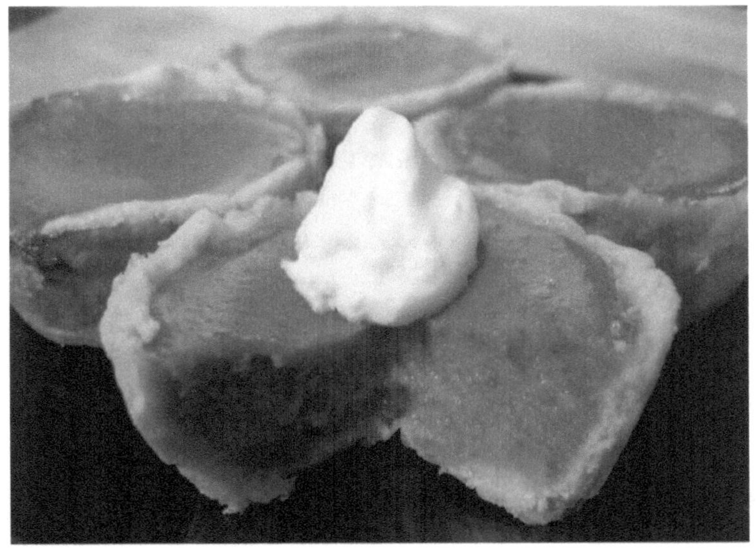

Yield: 12 Serving

Total Prep Time: 50 Minutes

List of Ingredients:

- 1 Bag of Pumpkin Spice Hershey Kisses
- 1 Cup of White Chocolate Chips
- 1 Can of Sweetened Condensed Milk
- ¼ Cup of Nutella
- ¼ Cup of Marshmallow Cream

XXXXXXXXXXXXXXXXXXXXXXXXXXXXXXXXXXXXXXXXXXXXXXXXXXX

How to Cook:

Melt the Condensed Milk and Chocolate Together.

Stir Until Smooth and Creamy.

Pour into A Paper Lined 8x8 Baking Dish.

Pour the Marshmallow Cream and Nutella Over The Top Of The Fudge.

Swirl in With A Knife.

Chill in The Fridge For 1 Hour.

Note: Serve Cold.

Recipe 4: Nutella Truffles

Yield: Unknown / depends on the ball size

Total Prep Time: 10 minutes

List of Ingredients:

- 1 cup of milk chocolate
- 2 tablespoons of Nutella
- ¼ cup of heavy cream
- Cocoa powder

xxxxxxxxxxxxxxxxxxxxxxxxxxxxxxxxxxxxxxxxxxxxxxxxxxxxxx

How to Cook:

1. Put heavy cream and milk chocolate to melt, meanwhile make sure you stir it every now and then.

2. Get a smooth creamy mixture.

3. Add Nutella into the mixture.

4. Cover the mixture with a transparent foil and put it in a fridge for 1 hour.

5. Take the mixture out of the fridge and start making tiny balls out of it.

6. Roll the balls into cocoa powder and serve them as you wish.

Note: You can replace the cocoa powder with something else, almonds, walnuts are a great choice.

Recipe 5: Nutella Strawberry Tart

Yield: 8 Servings

Total Prep Time: 45 Minutes

List of Ingredients:

For the Crust

- ½ cup of butter, cold
- ¼ cups sugar
- 1 tbsp of white wine vinegar
- 1 ½ cups flour

For the Filling

- 2 cups of milk
- 3/4 cup Nutella
- ½ teaspoons of vanilla extract
- ¼ teaspoons of hazelnut extract, optional
- 2 tbsp of cornstarch
- 1/8 teaspoon of salt
- 2-3 cups strawberries, cut in half

XXXXXXXXXXXXXXXXXXXXXXXXXXXXXXXXXXXXXXXXXXXXXXXXXXXX

How to Cook:

Preheat the Oven To 350 Degrees.

Mix Up Sugar and Flour in A Bowl.

Add Butter and The Vinegar and Stir Until Nicely Combined.

Put the Dough Out into A Tart Pan.

Press with Your Hands Carefully.

Bake For 20-25 Minutes.

Cool Before Filling.

Start Making the Filling Mixture.

Mix the Cornstarch And ¼ Cup of Milk in Another Bowl.

Add The 1 3/4 Cup of Milk, Nutella, Salt, And Extract to The Pan.

Stir Over Medium Heat Until the Nutella Completely Melts, Then Pour in The Cornstarch Mixture.

After Boiling, Stir For 2 Minutes and Slowly Pour It on The Crust.

Refrigerate For 1 Hour.

Note: Top with Strawberries. Serve Cold.

Recipe 6: Nutella French Toast Rolls

Yield: 10 Nutella French toast rolls

Total Prep Time: 15 minutes

List of Ingredients:

- 10 toasts
- 10 tablespoons of Nutella
- 1 egg
- 2 tablespoons of milk
- ½ cup sugar
- 1 tablespoon of cinnamon
- 1-2 teaspoons of butter

XXXXXXXXXXXXXXXXXXXXXXXXXXXXXXXXXXXXXXXXXXXXXXXXXXXXXX

How to Cook:

1. Remove the crust from the toast

2. Roll the toast with a roller, but make sure you do it very gently so it does not break apart.

3. Place 1 tablespoon of Nutella on each toast, coat it and roll it up.

4. Press the roll a little bit so it sticks together nicely.

5. Take a bowl and put egg and milk together, mix it up.

6. Take a plate and mix up the sugar and cinnamon together.

7. Heat up the cooking pan and melt the butter.

8. Put each roll in the egg/milk mixture.

9. Place the rolls in the cooking pan and roast them as you wish.

10. Take the roasted rolls and roll them in the
sugar/cinnamon mixture.

Note: You can fill the rolls with cream cheese, chopped
strawberries, marmalade or some other filling as desired.

Recipe 7: Nutella Swirl Pumpkin Pie

Yield: 10 Servings

Total Prep Time: 55 Minutes

List of Ingredients:

For the Crust

- 1 and ½ cups of cookie crumbs
- 5 tbsp of melted unsalted butter (slightly cooled)
- 2 tbsp of sugar

For the Filling

- 2 cups of fresh pumpkin puree
- ½ cup of warm Nutella
- ½ cup of heavy cream
- ¼ teaspoons of nutmeg
- 1 ½ teaspoons of cinnamon
- ½ teaspoons of ground ginger
- 3 large eggs
- ½ cup of packed dark brown sugar
- ¼ teaspoons of ground cloves
- ½ teaspoons of salt
- ½ cup of warm Nutella

XXXXXXXXXXXXXXXXXXXXXXXXXXXXXXXXXXXXXXXXXXXXXXXXXXXX

How to Cook:

Preheat oven to 350°f.

Spray the pie dish with a nonstick spray.

Mix up cookie crumbs with melted butter and sugar until well combined.

Press the mixture with your hands into the pie dish.

Bake crust for 10 minutes and give it some time to cool.

Add all of the other ingredients: except Nutella and eggs in another bowl.

Pour the mixture on top of the pie crust.

Add spoons of Nutella on the top.

Take a spoon and create swirls.

Bake at 350°f for 40-45 minutes.

Note: serve only when completely cold.

Recipe 8: Express Nutella Cubes

Yield: 15.7x10.2 inch baking tray

Total Prep Time: 45 minutes

List of Ingredients:

- 4 eggs
- 2 cups of sugar
- 2 vanilla extracts
- ½ tablespoon of salt
- 4 tablespoons of Nescaffe
- 2 cups of buttermilk
- 1 cup of oil
- 3 cups of flour
- 2 teaspoons of baking powder
- 5 tablespoons of Nutella

XXXXXXXXXXXXXXXXXXXXXXXXXXXXXXXXXXXXXXXXXXXXXXXXXXXX

How to Cook:

1. Preheat the oven to 360°F.

2. Mix up eggs, sugar, vanilla extract, salt and Nescaffe.

3. Mix until you get a foam structure.

4. Add buttermilk and oil

5. Add the mix of flour and baking powder to the mixture. (Slowly)

6. Add 5 large spoons of Nutella to the mixture and keep it smooth.

7. Pour the prepared mixture to a 15.7x10.2 inch baking tray.

8. Bake the mixture for 30 minutes.

9. Let it cool off and then sprinkle it with powdered sugar.

Note: You can add a cup of coconut or walnuts to the cake. It goes well together.

Recipe 9: Nutella Cookie Roll-Ups

Yield: 32 Servings

Total Prep Time: 60 Minutes

List of Ingredients:

- 1 box of refrigerated pie crusts
- ⅔ cup of Nutella
- 1 tbsp of melted butter
- 1 ½ teaspoon of sugar

xxxxxxxxxxxxxxxxxxxxxxxxxxxxxxxxxxxxxxxxxxxxxxxxxxxxx

How to Cook:

Preheat the oven to 375°f.

Unroll 1 entire crust and spread half of the Nutella over the crust-

Cut crust into 16 triangle shapes.

Roll each triangle and create a crescent shape.

Put them on a large cookie sheet.

Gently top with melted butter and sprinkle with sugar.

Bake for 23 minutes until it becomes golden brown.

Recipe 10: Chocolate Nutella Cups

Yield: A full plate

Total Prep Time: 45 minutes

List of Ingredients:

- 8 oz. chocolate chips of your choice

XXXXXXXXXXXXXXXXXXXXXXXXXXXXXXXXXXXXXXXXXXXXXXXXXX

How to Cook:

1. Put chocolate chips into a bowl and put it into a microwave for 30 seconds.

2. Stir a couple of times and repeat the process at least twice.

3. Line mini muffin pan with cupcake liners.

4. Take a tablespoon of chocolate and pour it into the bottom of cupcake liners.

5. Dip a back of your spoon into chocolate and spread it on the sides of cupcake liners. (Do this in order to hold the remaining cream).

6. Repeat the process until all of the cupcake liners are covered with chocolate.

7. Put in the fridge for 20 minutes.

8. Take a spoonful of Nutella and put it into each cupcake liner.

9. Take remaining chocolate and cover the cupcake liners which were previously filled with Nutella.

10. Put in the fridge for 20 minutes.

Note: Milk chocolate and semi-sweet chocolate are a great choice too.

Recipe 11: Nutellotti

Yield: 15 Servings

Total Prep Time: 15 Minutes

List of Ingredients:

- 1 ½ cups of flour
- ⅔ cup of Nutella
- Nutella for filling
- 1 egg

XXXXXXXXXXXXXXXXXXXXXXXXXXXXXXXXXXXXXXXXXXXXXXXXXXX

How to Cook:

In a bowl mix up Nutella and the egg until smooth.

Add the flour and stir in order to get a smooth texture.

Create 15 balls.

Put them on a baking tray.

Create a hole at the centre of each ball, with your fingers or whatever suits you.

Bake in a preheated oven at 355°f for 10 minutes.

Fill the cookies with Nutella using pastry bag.

Note: Let Them Cool Down Before Serving.

Recipe 12: Nutella Swirled Banana Snack Cake

Yield: 9 servings

Total Prep Time: 45 minutes

List of Ingredients:

- ¼ cup Nutella
- 1 tablespoon baking powder
- 1 cup all-purpose flour
- 1 large egg
- ½ tablespoon cinnamon
- ½ tablespoon baking soda
- ¼ tablespoon salt
- ¼ cup unsalted butter, at room temperature
- 1/3 cup brown sugar, packed
- ½ tablespoon vanilla extract
- 1/3 cup buttermilk
- 3 ripe bananas, mashed
- ¼ cup pecan halves, toasted

XXXXXXXXXXXXXXXXXXXXXXXXXXXXXXXXXXXXXXXXXXXXXXXXXX

How to Cook:

1. Preheat the oven to 350°F

2. Combine flour, baking powder, baking soda, cinnamon and salt.

3. Beat butter and sugar until you have a light fluffy structure.

4. Add the butter/sugar mixture to the egg and vanilla and beat it all together until well combined.

5. Pour the mixture into a baking tray and top it with Nutella.

6. Swirl into the mixture using figure eight motions.

7. Sprinkle with pecans.

8. Put into the oven and bake for 35 minutes.

Note: Let the cake cool down before cutting it.

Recipe 13: Oreo Smash Nutella Cookies

Yield: 24 Cookies

Total Prep Time: 25 Minutes

List of Ingredients:

- ½ Cups of melted and cooled butter for 5 minutes
- ½ cup of Nutella
- 3/4 cup of brown sugar
- ¼ cup of sugar
- 1 teaspoon of vanilla extract
- 1 ½ cups all-purpose flour
- 1 egg (lightly beaten)
- 1 tablespoon of cocoa powder
- ½ teaspoon baking powder
- ½ teaspoon of salt
- ½ teaspoon of baking soda
- 9 crushed Oreo cookies

How to Cook:

Preheat the oven to 350°f.

Melt the butter in a bowl and slowly stir in the Nutella.

Add sugar, vanilla extract and brown sugar and stir until well combined.

Add the egg, and continue on gently stirring the mixture.

Take a bowl and mix up the flour, baking powder, cocoa powder, salt and baking soda.

Stir the flour mixture into a butter mixture.

After well combined, add the crushed oreo cookies.

Create 24 balls out of the cookie dough you just made.

Put on a cookie sheet giving each ball 2 inches of space.

Gently press them down.

Bake at 350°f for 10 minutes.

Note: you can add anything into this dough, almonds and hazelnuts are great too!

Recipe 14: Dark Nutella Muffins

Yield: 34-36 Muffins

Total Prep Time: 30 minutes

List of Ingredients:

- 2 cups of flour
- 1 cup of sugar
- 2 vanilla extracts
- 2 tablespoons of baking soda
- 4 large tablespoons of powdered cocoa
- 4 eggs
- 16 large tablespoons of oil
- 1.5 cup of milk
- Nutella (34-36 teaspoons)

XXXXXXXXXXXXXXXXXXXXXXXXXXXXXXXXXXXXXXXXXXXXXXXXXXXX

How to Cook:

1. Preheat the oven to 350°F.

2. Take a bowl and mix all of the dry Ingredients together, until you have a smooth mixture.

3. Take another bowl and mix all other Ingredients together.

4. Slowly start adding the mixture from the second bowl to the first bowl where you put all of the dry Ingredients.

5. Mix all of these Ingredients for 3-4 minutes.

6. Take 34-36 cupcake liners and start filling them with the mixture.

7. Make sure you fill them only to the halfway.

8. Use a teaspoon of Nutella and place it on top of the cupcake liners fillings you have previously made.

9. Take the mixture and cover the Nutella fillings so it is completely invisible.

10. Bake in previously preheated oven on 350°F.

Note: Nutella filling is optional but is probably one of the tastiest choices. You can try out chocolate chips, almonds, vanilla and much more!

Recipe 15: Banana Nutella Trifle

Yield: 4 Servings

Total Prep Time: 15 Minutes

List of Ingredients:

Oreo Crumble

- 10 oreo cookies
- 2 tablespoons of unsalted butter, melted

Whipped Cream

- ½ Cup of heavy cream
- ½ teaspoon of vanilla extract
- 2 tablespoons of powdered sugar

Nutella Cream

- ½ Cup of cream cheese
- 1/3 cup of nutella
- ½ cup of heavy cream
- ½ teaspoon of vanilla extract
- 1/3 cup of powdered sugar

xxxxxxxxxxxxxxxxxxxxxxxxxxxxxxxxxxxxxxxxxxxxxxxxxxx

How to Cook:

Crush the oreo cookies and pour the melted butter over them.

Stir until it is all well combined.

Place into a baking pan and bake for 7 minutes at 375°f.

Take a bowl and mix up the whipped cream together with vanilla extract and powdered sugar.

Beat until the cream doubles its size and becomes stiff.

Put in a fridge.

Take a bowl and mix up Nutella with cream cheese until smooth.

Slowly pour in the heavy cream and continue on mixing until well combined.

Let the entire mixture cool off for at least 2 hours in the fridge.

Fill the dishes with previously made fillings as you wish.

Recipe 16: Nutellicious Cookies

Yield: Depends on the cookie size

Total Prep Time: 10 minutes

List of Ingredients:

- 2 cups of flour
- ½ teaspoon of salt
- 2 teaspoons of baking powder
- 1 cup of Nutella
- ¼ cup of butter (softened)
- 1 cup of sugar
- 2 eggs (room temperature)
- 1 tablespoon of vanilla extract
- 1 tablespoon of cocoa powder
- ⅓ cup of milk
- 3 cups of hazelnuts (peeled, roasted and sliced)
- ½ cup of powdered sugar

XXXXXXXXXXXXXXXXXXXXXXXXXXXXXXXXXXXXXXXXXXXXXXXXXXXX

How to Cook:

1. Take a bowl and mix up the flour, baking powder and salt.

2. Take another bowl and mix up Nutella, sugar and butter.

3. Take a third bowl and mix up eggs, vanilla extract, cocoa powder, milk and half of the hazelnuts.

4. Add the first mixture into the second bowl and mix it all up very well.

5. Leave in the fridge for 1 hour.

6. Preheat the oven to 375°F.

7. Put the powdered sugar in a bowl and the rest of hazelnuts to another bowl.

8. Create the balls made out of the dough you had put into the fridge previously.

9. Roll them into the hazelnuts and then into the powdered sugar.

10. Place them on a baking tray leaving 1 inch of the space between each cookie.

11. Gently press the balls, creating the real cookie shape.

12. Bake for 10 minutes.

Note: Instead of hazelnuts, you can use almonds, walnuts and dry fruit.

Recipe 17: No Bake Nutella Pie

Yield: 1 Pie

Total Prep Time: 20 Minutes

List of Ingredients:

- 25 Oreo cookies (don't remove the filling)

- 5 tablespoons of butter, melted

- 1 cup of Nutella

- 1 cup of package cream cheese (room temperature)

- 1 cup of cool whip, thawed

XXXXXXXXXXXXXXXXXXXXXXXXXXXXXXXXXXXXXXXXXXXXXXXXXXX

How to Cook:

Start preparing the crust.

Crush the cookies in a zip-bag.

Stir the crushed cookies in a bowl together with melted butter.

Place into a pie plate and gently press it down.

Put in a freezer while preparing the filling.

Take a bowl and mix up Nutella and cream cheese.

Beat until smooth and creamy.

Add cool whip in and stir until there are no white streaks.

Pour over the crust and gently smooth out the top.

Refrigerate for 4 hours.

Note: let the pie sit still for at least 4 hours before slicing. Add chocolate chips or almonds on top if you wish.

Recipe 18: Banana Rolls with Nutella

Yield: As much as you wish

Total Prep Time: None

List of Ingredients:

- 2 bananas
- 2 tortillas
- 1 teaspoon of Nutella for each tortilla

How to Cook:

1. Place a tortilla on a plate and cover it with Nutella. The amount of Nutella is completely up to you.

2. Put a banana on top of the Nutella covering and start rolling it with tortilla.

3. Cut each roll into at least 5 tiny rolls and serve as a desert.

Note: This recipe is completely customizable and you can put many different things in, depending on what you feel like, strawberries, ice cream, anything!

Recipe 19: Nutella Mocha Latte

Yield: 1 Serving

Total Prep Time: 5 Minutes

List of Ingredients:

- 2 shots of espresso
- ½ cup of milk
- 1 tbsp of Nutella
- Cocoa powder

xxxxxxxxxxxxxxxxxxxxxxxxxxxxxxxxxxxxxxxxxxxxxxxxxx

How to Cook:

Stir the Nutella in the mug for 2 minutes.

Pour the hot espresso over the Nutella carefully.

Stir until the drink is completely smooth.

Microwave milk in a jar for 1-2 minutes.

Shake the jar until the milk became foamy at the top.

Pour in the hot milk, carefully.

Sprinkle with cocoa powder on the top.

Note: when taking jar out of the microwave, take a towel and put it around the jar, it can be quite hot.

Recipe 20: Nutella Crunch Ice Cream Cake

Yield: 10 inches cake tin

Total Prep Time: None

List of Ingredients:

- 2 cups of Nutella
- 1 cup of puffed rice
- 13 cups of vanilla ice cream

xxxxxxxxxxxxxxxxxxxxxxxxxxxxxxxxxxxxxxxxxxxxxxxxxxxxxxx

How to Cook:

1. Take a deep bowl, put Nutella and puffed rice and mix it all together at a low temperature to make the Ingredients unite.

2. Take a tray, and cover it with baking paper and pour the mixture. Place it in the freezer to cool well and tighten, but not to freeze completely.

3. Remove the ice cream from the freezer and leave it in the fridge to soften so much that it can be mixed, but it must not melt.

4. After 35 to 40 minutes, remove the Nutella mixture from the fridge and cut it into small pieces, if necessary, return to the freezer until the ice cream softens up.

5. When the ice cream has softened, remove all of the cake Ingredients from the freezer/fridge.

6. Put the softened ice cream in the large bowl that you have taken out of the freezer, add 3/4 of Nutella's mixture,

7. Put the rest to the freezer until you make a cake, you will need it to put it on top of the cake. Combine well with the soft ice cream.

8. When you are done making your cake, take the Nutella pieces out of the freezer and spread all over the top of your cake.

9. Return the entire cake with its cake tin back to the freezer for at least 4 to 6 hours, or best overnight, to completely freeze.

Note: Be careful with melting and softening the ice cream, press the cake very well so there are no air bubbles left inside.

Recipe 21: No Bake Nutella Fudge

Yield: 20 Servings

Total Prep Time: 30 Minutes

List of Ingredients:

- 2 cups of nutella
- ½ cup of butter (soft)
- 13/4 cups of powdered sugar
- ½ teaspoon of vanilla extract
- 1 cup of milk chocolate chips
- 1 tablespoon of butter (soft)

How to Cook:

Mix Nutella and butter with a mixer.

Beat until creamy and smooth.

Add sugar and vanilla extract.

Pour the Nutella mixture into an 8x8 pan.

Melt the chocolate chips.

Add the tablespoon of softened butter in and melt for additional 15 seconds.

Spread the chocolate over Nutella mixture.

Put into the fridge.

Note: Let It Cool Before Cutting into Squares.

Recipe 22: Coconut Nutella Cake

Yield: 10x14 inches baking tray

Total Prep Time: 25 minutes

List of Ingredients:

- 3 cups of yogurt
- 2 cups of sugar
- 1 cup of oil
- 1 cup of coconut flour
- 2 cups of flour
- 3 tablespoons of cocoa
- 2 teaspoons of baking soda
- 2 cups of heavy cream
- 9 tablespoons of Nutella

XXXXXXXXXXXXXXXXXXXXXXXXXXXXXXXXXXXXXXXXXXXXXXXXXXXX

How to Cook:

1. Preheat the oven to 375°F.

2. Mix yogurt and sugar, then add oil, coconut flour and flour mixed with cocoa and soda bicarbonate.

3. Mix it well, and then pour it into a baking tray coated with butter and flour.

4. Bake in the oven heated to 375°F, about 25 minutes.

5. Let it cool down.

6. Spread 5 tablespoons of Nutella over the biscuit.

7. Mix up the heavy cream with rest of the Nutella and spread it over the biscuit you previously covered with 5 tablespoons of Nutella.

8. Put into the fridge for 1-2 hours.

Note: Make sure the cake is well cooled, otherwise it will be very difficult to cut it properly.

Recipe 23: Chocolate-Hazelnut Bars

Yield: 24 Bars

Total Prep Time: 35 Minutes

List of Ingredients:

- 3/4 cup of Nutella
- 1 cup of unsalted butter (room temperature)
- 1/3 cup of chopped hazelnuts
- 1 egg yolk
- 1 cup of light-brown sugar
- 1 teaspoon of vanilla extract
- 2 cups of all-purpose flour
- ½ teaspoons of salt
- ¼ cup of chopped hazelnuts

XXXXXXXXXXXXXXXXXXXXXXXXXXXXXXXXXXXXXXXXXXXXXXXXXXX

How to Cook:

Preheat the oven to 350°f.

Coat the baking pan with nonstick cooking spray.

Mix up butter, sugar, egg yolk and vanilla in a bowl until well combined.

Add in flour, 1/3 cup of chopped hazelnuts, salt and stir until well combined.

Bake for 20 minutes.

Let it cool off.

Sprinkle the top with chocolate-hazelnuts and remaining hazelnuts.

Chill for 1 hour.

Note: Do Not Cut Before It Has Been in The Fridge.

Recipe 24: Nutella Brownie Cake

Yield: 5 people

Total Prep Time: 30 minutes

List of Ingredients:

- 4 tablespoons flour
- 4 tablespoons oil
- 4 tablespoons sugar
- 4 eggs
- 2 tablespoons of Nutella
- 2 tablespoons of cocoa
- 1 vanilla extract
- 1 baking powder
- 1 cup of chopped hazelnuts

XXXXXXXXXXXXXXXXXXXXXXXXXXXXXXXXXXXXXXXXXXXXXXXXXXXXXX

How to Cook:

1. Preheat the oven to 400°F.

2. Mix eggs with sugar.

3. Combine flour with baking powder, cocoa, vanilla extract and hazelnuts.

4. Mix flour with eggs, Nutella and oil.

5. Stir well.

6. Pour the mixture in the baking tray and bake in a heated oven at 400°F for 20 minutes.

Note: The mixture has to be very well mixed. You can add other things instead of hazelnuts, walnuts are great too!

Recipe 25: Chocolate Nutella Smoothie

Yield: 2

Total Prep Time: 5 Minutes

List of Ingredients:

- 1 cup of soymilk (or milk substitute)
- 3 tablespoons of Nutella
- ½ tablespoon of agave or 1/2 tablespoons of honey
- 1 tablespoon of cocoa powder
- 1 banana
- 2 cups of ice cubes

How to Cook:

Add all of the ingredients into a blender.

Blend until smooth and creamy.

Note: put in a fridge for 1 hour, it makes it even better!

Recipe 26: Nutella Hot Chocolate

Yield: 2 people

Total Prep Time: 15 minutes

List of Ingredients:

- 2 cups of milk
- 2 tablespoons of Nutella
- 1/8 teaspoon of sea salt
- Heavy Cream
- Caramel sauce
- Hazelnuts

XXXXXXXXXXXXXXXXXXXXXXXXXXXXXXXXXXXXXXXXXXXXXXXXXXX

How to Cook:

1. Heat up the milk, salt and Nutella.

2. Mix it all very well and wait for it to boil.

3. Pour the mixture into glasses or cups and decorate them with vanilla sticks, chocolate chips, anything you like.

Note: Do not let it boil for too long, as soon as it starts boiling you should take it off.

Recipe 27: Nutella Granola

Yield: 16

Total Prep Time: 50 Minutes

List of Ingredients:

- 6 cups of rolled oats
- ½cup of wheat germ
- ¼ cup of sunflower seeds
- ¼ cup of almonds, chopped
- ¼ cup of raisins
- ¼ cup of craisins
- ½ cup of brown sugar
- 3⁄4 cup of Nutella
- ½ cup of canola oil

xxxxxxxxxxxxxxxxxxxxxxxxxxxxxxxxxxxxxxxxxxxxxxxxxxx

How to Cook:

Combine 6 cups of rolled oats, ½ cup of wheat germ, ¼ cup of sunflower seeds and ¼ cup of chopped almonds in a bowl.

Heat up the Nutella, brown sugar, and oil in the microwave for about 1 minute.

Pour on the oatmeal mix and then stir to coat.

Spread onto an 11 x 15 inch cookie tray.

Bake at 450°f for two hours, stirring every 20 minutes.

Carefully take out of the oven and then toss in raisins/craisin.

Note: Let Them Cool Completely.

Recipe 28: Nutella Doughnuts

Yield: 12 people

Total Prep Time: 60 minutes

List of Ingredients:

- 2 cups of flour
- 1 cup of yeast
- ¾ cup of warm milk
- ¼ cup of sugar
- ¼ teaspoon of salt
- 2 teaspoons of butter (room temperature)
- 2 egg yolks
- ⅛ cup of powdered sugar
- 2 tablespoons of Nutella
- 2-3 tablespoons of hot water

XXXXXXXXXXXXXXXXXXXXXXXXXXXXXXXXXXXXXXXXXXXXXXXXXX

How to Cook:

1. Pour warm milk in the bowl, add the sugar and yeast and leave for a few minutes.

2. Take a bowl and put flour and salt, create a hole in the middle and add butter, egg yolk and yeast you used in step 1.

3. Cover the mixture with aluminum foil and let it sit still for 1 hour.

4. After the dough is good enough, start creating the famous doughnuts.

5. Roll the dough ½ inch thick and cut it with a glass or a doughnut mold.

6. Cover your doughnuts and let them sit still for 30 minutes.

7. Heat up the oil and start making your doughnuts.

8. Each side of the doughnut should be 1 minute in the oil.

9. To make the chocolate Nutella covering, you need to take a bowl and prepare the mixture.

10. Put powdered sugar, Nutella and hot water in a bowl.

11. Stir until you get a tasty and shiny mixture.

12. Dip one side of your doughnuts into the Nutella mix.

Note: You can decorate the doughnuts with chocolate chips, confetti and much more!

Recipe 29: Nutella Mousse

Yield: 8 Servings

Total Prep Time: 15 Minutes

List of Ingredients:

- 1 cup of heavy cream
- ¼ teaspoon of instant coffee granules
- ½ cup of Nutella
- Whipped cream - optional

XXXXXXXXXXXXXXXXXXXXXXXXXXXXXXXXXXXXXXXXXXXXXXXXXXX

How to Cook:

Mix up heavy cream and instant coffee granules.

Stir for at least 5 minutes.

Add nutella.

Beat with a mixer for 2-3 minutes.

Note: let it cool off for at least 4 hours before serving. Top with whipped cream right before serving.

Recipe 30: Fast Nutella Cake

Yield: 3 people

Total Prep Time: 10 minutes

List of Ingredients:

- 2 cups of Nutella
- 6 eggs

XXXXXXXXXXXXXXXXXXXXXXXXXXXXXXXXXXXXXXXXXXXXXXXXXXX

How to Cook:

1. Preheat the oven to 350°F.

2. Break the eggs into a bowl and mix it for 6 minutes.

3. Take the two cups of Nutella and put it in a microwave to melt.

4. Do not melt it completely, just so it is not hard.

5. Stir the Nutella into the egg mixture three times and get a smooth tasty mixture.

6. Pour the entire mixture into a baking tray (small one) and bake until you can see a really nice crust on top.

Note: Do not cut the cake before it cools down.

About the Author

Heston Brown is an accomplished chef and successful e-book author from Palo Alto California. After studying cooking at The New England Culinary Institute, Heston stopped briefly in Chicago where he was offered head chef at some of the city's most prestigious restaurants. Brown decide that he missed the rolling hills and sunny weather of California and moved back to his home state to open up his own catering company and give private cooking classes.

Heston lives in California with his beautiful wife of 18 years and his two daughters who also have aspirations to follow in their father's footsteps and pursue careers in the culinary arts. Brown is well known for his delicious fish and chicken dishes and teaches these recipes as well as many others to his students.

When Heston gave up his successful chef position in Chicago and moved back to California, a friend suggested he use the internet to share his recipes with the world and so he did! To date, Heston Brown has written over 1000 e-books that contain recipes, cooking tips, business strategies for catering companies and a self-help book he wrote from personal experience.

He claims his wife has been his inspiration throughout many of his endeavours and continues to be his partner in business as well as life. His greatest joy is having all three women in his life in the kitchen with him cooking their favourite meal while his favourite jazz music plays in the background.

Author's Afterthoughts

Thank you to all the readers who invested time and money into my book! I cherish every one of you and hope you took the same pleasure in reading it as I did in writing it.

Out of all of the books out there, you chose mine and for that I am truly grateful. It makes the effort worth it when I know my readers are enjoying my work from beginning to end.

Please take a few minutes to write an Amazon review so that others can benefit from your opinions and insight. Your review will help countless other readers make an informed choice

Thank you so much,

Heston Brown